Lifescapes

Lifescapes

Poems by

Lee Woodman

Cover design by Shay Culligan
Author photograph by Sonya Melescu

ISBN: 978-1-954353-50-3

Kelsay Books
502 South 1040 East, A-119
American Fork, Utah, 84003

for Bill Kircher
and
Stephanie Cotsirilos

with deep thanks

Acknowledgments

Many thanks to the publications in which versions of the following poems have appeared:

Poets Choice Publishing: "Chocolate Crescendos," "Orchid," "Spirits," "Secrets I Tell Myself"
The Ekphrastic Review: "In Which I Consider Myself a Possible Woman of Algiers"
The Hill Rag: "What to Expect at Congressional Cemetery"
Tiferet Journal: "Story Tower," "Cento"
vox poetica: "Sort of American Haiku for a Catskill Mountain Home," "Strange Currency," "Essence of Blackbird"

Contents

Vermilion Suit   15
Can You Live with Ambiguity?   17
What I Learned in Australia   19
Fish Hearth   21
Story Tower   23
Orchid   25
Heart Failure   26
It Was Different than Fainting   29
Waiting   30
A Rebirth   34
When Parents Go Away   35
Cento: The Self, the Soul, the Body   36
No More Sugar   37
Modern Day Houdinis   38
Shah Jehan and Mumtaj: It Takes Two   39
Meditations on Sensations   40
Secrets Between an Actress and a Prostitute   42
In Which I Consider Myself a Possible Woman of
    Algiers   45
Chocolate Crescendos   48
Sort of American Haiku for a Catskill Mountain
    Home   49
Zodiac   50
Spirits   51
Her Collections   52
Secrets I Tell Myself   53
Signposts   55
Wake-up Call   56
Advent   57
2020 Upheaval   58
What to Expect at Congressional Cemetery   60
A Wounded Pastoral   62

Running Refrains in Choleric Times   63
Digital Divorce   64
Essence of Blackbird   65
Strange Currency   67
Castles in the Air   68
Divorce Prayer: In Perpetuity Throughout the
    Universe   70

Vermilion Suit

Friday-night tired, drifting,
I almost did not pick up.
Your voice, very purposeful,
Hello? You answered my ad,
Pediatrician, passion for the arts...?

The conversation rising,
we settled on a meeting at the Plaza
the following Monday.
How will I know you?
My vermilion suit, I answered.

You had to say yes, whether you knew
it was a color or not.
A tiny corner nook, upscale bar,
two glasses of Pinot Grigio,
teeny dish of salty cashews.

First impressions crossed our foreheads;
questions circled our ears.
You were reading Amitav Ghosh;
I grew up in Bangalore. You were fond
of museums; I worked at the Met.

Why I dared accept a ride, I do not know.
You dropped me off suggesting that
you'd enjoy doing something cultural,
which sounded vaguely sexual.
We went to the Guggenheim.

Each anniversary we always arrived
separately, strangely nervous.
7 PM, October 18th, same hotel
for twenty years. Still vermilion.
Still wondering,

Will I know you?

Can You Live with Ambiguity?

You asked if I could live with ambiguity.
That was quite some time after we met by want-ad
where you wrote "pediatrician, arts and ideas."
That caught my attention and I responded.

It was quite some time after we met by want-ad;
you said you'd like to do something edifying.
That caught my attention and I responded.
We drove to Brooklyn in your pale blue Buick.

You said you'd like to do something edifying.
There was a lot of press about a dark German film;
we drove to Brooklyn in your pale blue Buick.
You talked about archetypes; I spoke of characters.

There was a lot to say about that dark German film;
the notion of schadenfreude was unsettling.
We talked about personalities, odd film characters.
I asked if you were serious about a life-time mate.

The notion of schadenfreude was unsettling.
You had three sons but delayed my meeting them.
I asked if you were serious about a life-time mate—
caution ruled your world, but you met me in Berlin.

You had three sons but revealed them slowly.
I sensed you were a tiger, fiercely protecting your cubs—
caution ruled your world, but you met me in Berlin.
You described your irate mother, absent tight-lipped father.

I learned you were a tiger, fiercely protecting your cubs,
yet your gentle delight in opera, jazz, and fine arts turned my heart.
Did you resemble your irate mother, absent tight-lipped father?
Avid reader, successful pediatrician…surely, you must be caring.

17

Your pure delight in opera, jazz, and fine arts turned my heart.
But money, o yes money. Could we ever come to mesh?
Avid reader, successful pediatrician...surely, you must be caring.
Pre-nup, children, wills—we needed outside counsel.

But money, o yes money. Would we ever come to mesh?
Marriage seemed appealing, but life presented clashes.
Pre-nup, children, wills—we needed outside counsel.
I yearned for self-driving cars; you wanted everything the same.

Marriage seemed appealing, but life presented clashes.
My desire for the beach was countered by your mountains.
I yearned for self-driving cars; you wanted everything the same.
I pressed for travel, guests, and swimming nude at midnight.

The mountains versus beach gave way to mostly mountains.
I danced less, hardly swam; you were stern, in bed at ten.
I pressed for travel, guests, and swimming nude at midnight.
Affection was conditional; we muddled in sex but carried on.

I danced less, hardly swam; you turned out lights at ten.
I fell low in your ranking of profession, money, family.
Affection was conditional; we muddled in sex and carried on.
You did ask once if I could live with ambiguity.

What I Learned in Australia

An apologetic phone message: "The tour van broke down,"
seconded by a note at the front desk.

I was thrilled, glad for a day unplanned on my own
to wander throughout the harbor front.

I took a cloudy picture of the Sydney Opera house;
I already had a sunny one, the classic.

When you're alone, thoughts become unruly,
uninvited memories demand your attention.

Plenty of time to climb the staircase of the art museum
where I could ponder a simple piece:

white letters etched into grey granite boldly declaring,
It's Such a Thin Line Between Clever and Stupid.

I almost wanted to marry Brad, but the wine stain he left
on my white carpet while I slept was bloody garnet.

More art at the harbor, where a sculptor's poem echoed,
Under Your Mind Lies a Tunnel.

We know things before we know them truly. At the 10K,
he met a runner with a tattoo. She must have loved pot.

At the aquarium, I admired zebra seahorses and blue angelfish,
amazed these two species could both be fish.

Alone at the hotel bar that night, I drank a dry martini
and began two poems,

not about koalas, tacludas, gray kangaroos, or red sands,
not about the luminescence of opals—

a sestina about my former lover Brad who lied,
and a pantoum about you, who probably didn't.

Fish Hearth

On land,
horrible things happen—
a breach of trust.
Brad told me he slept with her.

My muddled mind
anguished with imagined details—
they met at a race,
her shapely legs glistening,
her long limbs, nude muscled beauties.

They did not hesitate to lie
together on the scarlet quilt I had given him.
Not long after he disappeared, I learned
she had moved in.
Already two names on the voicemail,
they were happy.

When I am sad,
I sink under water,
glide forward,
lids open wide.
Water flushes cool,
washing past my hot face,
pushing me past thousands
of tiny shimmering fish.

Shoals of see-through silversides
surround me. I am one of theirs.
Swimming in unison approaching the light,
our underbodies glow white.

My feet merge into a tiny forked tail,
my arms into two dorsal fins.
I must stay here, forming, reforming
until I can rise on my own.

Story Tower

*inspired by Nikolai Rimsky-Korsakov's
"Scheherazade," the music and the story*

Building story on story
Balcony by balcony
Windows with blinds—

        We frame our lives

Four oboes take us forward,
We heed recurring themes
A river flows unwinding

        with currents underneath

The leavings too familiar,
Arpeggios gone rogue
Each day a chapter lengthens,

        each year the epic grows

We deflect, we hide in labor,
Five trumpets push us on
We raise the shades of mourning,

        a seed becomes a rose

We soften as two harps wrap
Around the violins
Torment melts to forgiveness

        reprise becomes reprieve

There's a rhythm to our days now,
Remorse and anguish end
We know this lilting story

        we climb the stairs again

We need one thousand stories,
To fall in love so slowly
A tender piccolo's refrain—

        standing on balconies, I remain

Orchid

The orchid is perfect,
climbing the stake, tall
and straight; it unfolds
and arches over,
with four bright blossoms
and pale green buds that
promise to grow.
Pink petals inside white,
golden tendrils inside pink
wave—tickling the air,
awaiting company.
I arch my back on
silken sheets.
His breath is slow;
there is only endless time.
Warm fingers travel
the arch, nuzzling over
creamy hill and
strawberry nipple,
trailing downward
to softening petals below.
What once was cool melts
with a promise of lush oil.
As stem meets blossom,
tendrils tremble and yield to
sweet pain.

Heart Failure

To come home is to enter serene space:
our pale jade rugs, velvet swivel chairs,
Tommy Flanagan on the radio.

Friday, your late night, I'll be home earlier,
bathe in salts, pull on a sea-green fleece,
pad around the rooms in furry slippers.

Plenty of time till 8 PM—
we'll eat poached salmon and kale,
sitting close on the gold-flecked bench.

A block away a homeless woman
with scarred hands searches for a cot
at a neighborhood shelter.

Hoarse coughs from her sunken chest
resound through the boarding house.
She'll be put outside again tomorrow.

I glance at the clock, disbelieving.
It's already 9! Where are you?
My stomach starts turning, I run

to my study, the answering machine
blinking. I hear your taped message:
"…in the ER. Please come soon."

I hit erase by mistake.
Shaky legs stumbling, I grope
for my coat and keys,

trip down the stairs to the car,
pull out onto dark city streets.
I hope you said Mt. Sinai.

On the cross street, I find
a parking space, whisper "Sweet Jesus."
A nurse waits; the doctor motions.

I feel nothing, not my feet walking, not my
heart throbbing, into the gauze of ER space.
There on the gurney, shrunken, gray-white,

is an alive you—breathing comfortably.
The doctors feed you massive doses of
Naproxen, want to watch you overnight.

You cough intermittently, but less
than the tuberculin woman I heard before.
I wipe sweat from your forehead.

They expect a viral infection, inflamed
heart muscle. Carvedilol might help.
The salmon and the kale have died;

I don't know about the woman.
At home, I call your patients letting
them know you'll be out for a while.

You know I'll help you heal—
I'll prop you in the swivel chair,
feed you tuna fish, nuts, cheese.

As long as I have strength
to hold us both up, we're ok;
it has always been that way.

I am the one most changed.

It Was Different than Fainting

inspired by C. D. Wright

It's not what you imagine. How darkness
covers. You can't know, can you? You pay attention
to something else: then it happens, while you're watching.
A moment before concussion, total
concentration on a task, a careful task, the grasping
for a grandchild's hand, you step from the tub.
Resounding thud, head to ledge, lower teeth rattle.
You search for sight, yet only hear the child singing.
O athlete—   No longer
will you be surefooted on the track—no more
will you take two steps at a time.
Between composing countless stanzas, you left
the web of family. Blackness drove
the lights out. You must know it could happen,
flash of a second—the before, the after of forever.

Waiting

inspired by Elizabeth Bishop

A man ahead of me in line
pronounces his Nigerian
name, trying to convince
the clerk he has insurance,
does not need a referral.
Purell dispenser below
the wide TV screen, CNN
commentator counting
all the Trump firings.
PEOPLE
magazine (dog-eared),
declares *Prince Harry and
Meghan Markle
'Moving Out.'* Moving
out of what?

All at once, Howard
looms over me, loudly
Please follow!
He goes through the drill—
*Changes in medication?
Changes in vision?*
Instead of saying *You
mean Vision?* I struggle
to read the chart.
I wonder if he knows
the whole world—
vision, marriage—
has changed.

No surprise when my voice
becomes the reporter's:
We're airlifted by Elon Musk,
trapped by Ebola, cyber-

struck by China.
Shrinking world,
all planets topsy-turvy,
unpredictable. Terrifying.

Life changing crises—
unexpected as
concussion, retinal
hole, damaged optic nerve.
Unexpected as
age spots outnumbering
freckles, or a mirror
showing a crag settle
between the lip and chin.
Horrifying as a partner
going silent, sullen.

My heart is uncertain,
my anger convulsive.
My feet walk ahead
of my brain,
my vision is where?
Margaret Mead determined
there should be time-limited
relationships: one
for childbearing, one for
profession, one for old age.

Dr. Long appears, my
pupils fully dilated.
What's new? he chirps.
No words come,
but I understand Harry
and Meghan, how they
smile out loud and
hide inside.

He checks pressure,
cataracts. Just like last
time, he says,
*The retina looks
very good. I'd like
to check again in
another six months.*

Whose six months?

He forgets I can't read
properly. He did not
check the optic nerve—
not his universe.

The sun is too bright
when I try to drive.
I cannot decipher the
signs on the GPS; world
solstices are slipping.

My sister thinks it
may be the Apocalypse—
Iran, Pakistan, bombs,
a school kid run amok,
world water contamination.

Back to the check-out desk
where patients pay
without question, I don
plastic glare protectors
for dilated pupils.

Viewing life anew
requires throwing the
pickup sticks, tossing
out patterns,
creating a cataclysm—
the continents must break
apart—go dark.
I will come back only
via tectonic shift.

A Rebirth

I thought I was born on a Friday, September 25th.
My mother said I was induced at the Boston Lying-In.
I find on the Internet that it was really a Saturday, and
wonder if she forgot what day it was.

Years ago, I found my way to a vestry basement,
West End Lutheran Church.
Notice of a séance on Sunday afternoon:
Experience Rebirth! Two experts will guide you!

Lying on the floor, belly-up, I performed breathing exercises.
The trance started in the second phase of forceful
panting, the fall started before the exhalation was over:
visions, hallucinations, my hands and limbs shook.

An image of mom in my third eye—she was the one
seeking oblivion. Her doctor agreed to induce her,
a vogue of birth at that time. No other plans
for that Friday, unconsciousness to be short-lived.

And, I was born.

Something is lost when teased, enticed, forced out.
A child must flip upside down, be cajoled to come,
have a cord cut at someone else's bidding. In rebirth,
you lose a day of your life. Perhaps a Friday.

When Parents Go Away

What haunted me
for years is true.
Young Carol and I
return from a party,
cross the courtyard
of her parents'
home, see the bathroom
door ajar. Her sister,
Anna, sunk in the tub,
wrists sliced open,
sickish coral-pink
water. Frantic parents
stumble into the car,
Carol sobbing
in the back seat,
Anna wrapped
in blankets,
dead glassy stare.
And then,
they're all gone.

Hours later when
they return,
Anna is alive,
both forearms
bound thick with gauze.
Car doors open,
horrified mother gasps.
She realizes they
left me
in the driveway
alone.
I was still there,
clutching my wrists.

Cento: The Self, the Soul, the Body

after Sylvia Plath, William Carlos Williams,
John Ashbery, Gerard Manley Hopkins,
Elizabeth Bishop, William B. Yeats,
Stephen Dunn, and Sharon Olds

Standing on their shoulders, I listen to all the voices chant:

I am the arrow…

In a case like this, I know quick action is the main thing.

I don't understand myself, only segments of myself that
misunderstand each other—

(I sit) *on meadow and river and wind-wandering and weed-*
winding bank,

one foot of the sun steadies itself,

(and) *as I cast out remorse,*

so great a sweetness flows into the breast.

We must laugh, and we must sing.

No one should ask the other, "What were you thinking?"

I lie there in the air as if flying rapidly without moving, and slowly
I cool off.

No More Sugar

He left me for the first time when our refrigerator broke down—
food went bad, frozen stuff smelled vile. No help.

No offer to pick me up at the airport after a business trip. *Your
company pays for travel and meals, right?* Where was the sweet
reunion?

When I was in pain, no melting to say, *Oh, baby, I'm sorry I hurt
you,* just a slow dissolve of communication. The zest fell flat.

His coach beat him, apologized, then beat him again.
How can he forgive, trust? He can't blend. Too much stirring.

No digesting the kids' problems together—filial envy, raw
jealousy, a child who doesn't eat. He can't weigh or measure; I
have no recipes.

Rigid bedtime hour, stricter menu regimen. What happened to
bourbon after theater, ice cream and TV? Soon we'll just live on
air, scant water.

After all these years, we are non-stick pans. No baking, microwave
silence. Angers, like off-kilter mixing bowls, spin out of orbit.

Modern Day Houdinis

Both magicians make choices, their tricks getting
harder and harder, their escapes more daring.

Swallow one hundred needles with a small drink of water,
pull them from your gut in a frayed knotted string.

One of us channels David Copperfield, dancing his
way to dollars and prominence,

not noticing illusions that got left behind,
not expecting to be called to court for negligence.

We are Penn and Teller—one emotes, bleats;
the other retreats, emits nothing.

The edges of our play list got burned;
that's how a fire dies, the sheaf of paper collapses.

There is no more kindling for the heart to grab,
no more oxygen to uphold the stage.

We have cut each other in half, severed a common core,
extinguished strong flames with downpours of tears.

Trying to live in the same tank of water,
we each must save our self before drowning together.

Shah Jehan and Mumtaj: It Takes Two

A couple well-known as iconic:
he rich, she artistic—harmonic.

Ruthless king named her "Queen of the Castle";
his other wives gave him no hassle.

Main interest for him—architecture—
obsessed with his work, infrastructure.

But, she wanted guest rooms for artists—
astrologers, poets, sitarists.

Planned closets for him full of uniforms,
playrooms for children with unicorns.

The world only knew of their love-match,
hardly noticed her grief when he detached,

taking granted her grace and compassion,
while his focus was all war and mansions.

Jealous her fame was growing apace,
(she did wield great power in affairs of state)

Plot her demise? He had killed his two brothers.
Neglect her poor health, plan her death as a mother?

Rumors remain—the story mysterious—
which victim suffered blows more injurious?

The alive one can weep, build tombs in her memory;
the dead can come forth, through a life extrasensory.

Meditations on Sensations

after Robert Hass's "Meditations
at Lagunitas"

All old thinking is about fond memories. New
thinking is about experiencing the present, living
in the moment, reconstructing memories. Essentially,
you are part of the mass universe of bodies, celestial
and otherwise, creating a conscious feeling:

Perhaps you are in a yoga pose, say Virabhadrasana II,
pressing hard on the supporting back heel, some
age-old stretch over time like all warriors.
Or, you heed the voice of an eight-year-old girl pronouncing
instructions about breakfast juice: *Close your eyes and make*
your brain think of banana, then strawberry, then orange.
You'll taste them all.

I thought about that at "The Nutcracker" when listening
to the orchestra: taste the harp, tap the
castanets, draw a gut bow across violins. I
understood that everything can taste, feel, sound—
experience, beauty, bitterness, damaged hearts, helpless children.

There was a moment at Tanglewood, morning dance
class with Clyde Morgan, when after performing pliés
for years, I felt my first plié, the long interior thighs
of second position, the slow descent, torso rising in opposition,
all muscles pulling their weight. My knees splayed,
my feet firm, my torso one spine-knob atop the next
through my neck and head—plié. I had been
dancing for sixteen years, yet learned something so old so newly.

We have been married for nineteen years. I long to learn what we
have practiced all this time. A lost art, more than a leg bend.
Too much going on in the head, a brain can only work so hard.
Do you remember how to touch, taste, see me?
Make me forget my body, only the tingling.

Secrets Between an Actress and a Prostitute

Carlotta is in the window seat; I take the aisle.
She orders bourbon, no ice.
Skin-tight gold lamé pants, bronze angora sweater.
Zirconia rings circle every finger and two toes.
Despite being winter in Monterey, she wears spiky sandals,
toenails flashing dark purple polish, sparkly appliqués.
As the plane takes off, I glance at her face:
layers of pancake make-up, jet black curled eyelashes, fierce.
She is 50 or 80, high teased hair.
Honeyed locks, highlighted with swaths of caramel,
pulled back into a ponytail.
I make her a prostitute.

The captain blocks music to our earphones.
He announces altitude, ETA in Houston,
names of service attendants in first class cabin and coach.
During this reprieve, I make up my actress name,
plays I've been in, summer stock locations.
While I'm served coffee, she asks and I introduce
myself as Lily Rousseau, quickly naming
roles I've played in: *Annie Get Your Gun,*
Anna and the King of Siam, Sound of
Music. All plays with controlling men.

Carlotta and I share nothing in common
except this leg of the journey—
five hours to Houston, plenty of time
for lite chat with a stranger.
I learn about four husbands, sizeable inheritance,
her marble-paved driveway and Mary Kay Cadillacs.
She is far from a wench—doctorate in economics,
father in real estate. Flabbergasted to learn
she was educated in an elite prep school,

I find it hard to imagine this woman
in plaid skirts, knee socks, and loafers—
she makes a convincing casino Madam.

Carlotta's starts to question me:
Why theater? Do you like impersonating people
you could never be in real life?
How did you train your voice, learn to dance?
It must be hard for your husband when you
are away most nights.
Lily is a bit dumbstruck. But it's much easier
to respond with conjured answers rather than real.
Imposter syndrome invades my mind.
Some would say I'm an artist; others, a businesswoman.
Acquaintances think I'm an extrovert; friends
recognize the private side. Men describe me as resilient,
strong; women admire my creativity, willingness to risk.
To the outside world, I am a settled wife,
partner in a perfect marriage.

The plane bumps, rocks.
Stewardesses race down the aisle calling
for all to buckle seatbelts.
Overhead luggage bins fly open,
suitcases slide back and forth. Tubes with masks drop,
swing near our noses. Bourbon, coffee, ranch dressing
spray across nubby blue headrests. Captain comes on
loudspeaker, announces there is significant turbulence
ahead. We already know that.

Then, the calm.
Relief. Smooth sailing for a while.
Amazing to see how fast the flight attendants restore order.
They've been here before, know exactly what they're doing,
exactly who they are.

I want to be myself now, no more talking with Carlotta.
I check to make sure my purse is safe, look for my license,
verify my real name. I don't have to be someone new yet;
there is still time to think a separation over.
After a few moments of closing my eyes, meditating
through rising and falling breaths, I peek at Carlotta.
She's checking her purse too. Perfectly calm,
she scans the stub for the next leg of her journey.
Turns out she's not terminating in Houston at all,
not heading back to Monterey. She's rerouting to Vegas.

I search for twilight imagery: nametags, my old red sweater
from Anthropologie, keys to the apartment where we have
lived so long, if you will be home when I get there,
if you can read my mind.

In Which I Consider Myself a Possible Woman of Algiers

after Eugène Delacroix's "The Women of Algiers in their Apartment," 1834

Delacroix, like me, is charmed but deluded,
fascinated by their harem allure—
luscious flesh, bejeweled bodices,
vibrant costumes, figs.

Entering through swinging saloon doors,
I pose for them.
My red bloomers are brighter than theirs;
my cheeks burn violet energy.

They do not look my way;
I am disturbing the languor, familiar stupor.
Leaning on thick rugs, bolstered pillows,
these plump doyennes are adorned

with gold necklaces that sparkle against
nude chests, coyly covered by see-
through muslin blouses.

Turkish turned-up sandals,
thrown to the side, reveal
meaty feet, pudgy toes.
At times, our ladies shift positions
to ease a hip or elbow—

discomfort does not suit them.
Bored with the hookah,
they compare the men
they bedded last night:

45

a corpulent prince with lacquered hair;
sanctimonious merchant, smelling of musk;
odoriferous suitor, stale wine, spunk.

Spiritless, they wait uncounted hours;
tomorrow night will be a repeat.
Blue-black Algerian servant,
Samia, turns away from them,
she's heard it all before.

The mirror on the tiled wall above them
tilts forward; she has not bothered
to straighten it.

She stops abruptly when she sees me.
Am I a new consort?
She determines not;
we are kindred spirits she and I—

different kinds of gems.
We recognize this luxuriant space as dark;
light shines through a depressed window
but to no end.

It doesn't appear to go anywhere,
only opens to the kitchen
where Samia is headed.
I believe it leads to Exodus;
we could run fast, holding hands

to escape this confinement.
As I attempt to find my way to her
across the circle of ladies,
a putrid smell rises—

moths in the drapes, cockroaches
in the corner—sad truth exhaling
from the rotten flesh of women
under those bloomers.

Dressed-up dolls, dulled by men
who tell them they are well-taken care of,
don't realize their pearl anklets,
endless hashish, servants-in-waiting

keep them prisoners for life.
I pick my way through an airless world
across plush carpets to follow brave Samia.

At least, Delacroix had foresight to render her
with fleet feet and shoes on.

Chocolate Crescendos

Warm melting
dark chocolate
graham crust
crème fraiche.

Shared with a friend,
downed with cappuccino,
swirls of foamy milk.

Once at Barachou with you long ago,
I had a chocolate torte which I never forgot,
and yet here I taste something better.

perfectly moist
soothing
easy to spoon out.

Reminds me of clearing clouds that welcome sun,
late afternoon on the dock, lazy summer.
I won't go home to cook dinner.

Lie here,
sip Cointreau,
tip one more teaspoon,
soft Cadbury to my tongue.

Sort of American Haiku for a Catskill Mountain Home

inspired by Allen Ginsberg

I've been enchanted and beguiled by eager shrubs known to survive short summers, bedazzled by "volunteer" naturals blown over by wind

Purple lupine, trillium, dangling Solomon's Seal.

I've been overtaken and outmaneuvered by a sloping hill in back, clear-cut one hundred years ago, now teeming with red spruce and chokecherry suffocated by

Bittersweet.

I've been outpaced and defeated by weeds in the path. Stony unpaved gravel roadway, nicely rolled in May, now cheers on

Bull Thistle, Oxalis.   *Crabgrass.*

Zodiac

Our problem, born earthbound, extends outward to the universe.
We counted on permanence, then meteors hit.
Marriage eclipsed by a fall while caring for children—
concussion of stars, I only blinked black.
We were sunspots of life, headed toward twilight. But
conversations ended; two quasars quit. A polite death.
A galaxy of unspoken regrets, he was light-years gone—
what animal comes next in my zodiac?
Here, I am a balanced Libra. In China, I am a rat.

Spirits

Call me Hecate, I travel by night,
my broom casting spells upon men.
They wonder why I must take flight.

Compare me to fleet Aphrodite,
crooning love songs as she ascends.
Call me Hecate, I travel by night

to conjure new schemes I raise to incite,
aware that the change I require offends.
Small wonder that I must take flight.

Antigone warns by sharing foresight
how women can stand unrepentant.
Call me Hecate, I travel by night.

Explore! rebel!   To create is my right.
I need warriors, willing kings to attend,
not wonder why I must take flight.

Harken the wild man, the lover and knight
who pushes me higher, delights in my pen.
Call me Hecate, I travel by night, as
darkness descends, I bloom and take flight.

Her Collections

She never collected anything:
No coins, no stamps, no butterflies
No hats, shoes or scarves (well maybe scarves)
No political buttons or cars or trains
Definitely no Santa Clauses or reindeer statues
No Russian dolls or eggs

The truth is she loves getting rid of stuff:
       All the old videos and films
       All the files from jobs long outdated
       All the labels that have lost their sticky
       All chipped china and glassware
       A parade of men

She does have one small Waterford elephant.
Nothing more to get rid of.
Two large rooms, two floor-to-ceiling windows
Gleaming parquet, one maple table.
Plenty of light.

Secrets I Tell Myself

When I was ten,
my friend Stephanie and I tore ends from a foam pillow
to make breasts we did not have

When I was thirteen,
I held my wrists in bed at the Honolulu Hotel
so I would not commit suicide by mistake

When I was sixteen,
I lay on the bathroom tiles feeling my stomach, my heart
thumped in my abdomen, I feared I was pregnant

When I was twenty,
I weighed 88 pounds and hid prune yogurt
in the cooler of the dance studio at college

When I was a dancer at Tanglewood,
I'm sure a famous composer
put Quaaludes in my Kool-Aid

During my first marriage,
I told my mother-in-law if her wonderful son
and I ever separated, we'd be good friends

When I got pregnant
by my first husband after we separated,
I told no one and insisted on abortion within a week

When I drank clear vodka for three nights
after being stalked by a schizophrenic Jesus freak
I did not tell my third husband it was not water

As I am nearing seventy,
I tell myself these secrets
and repeat them to see if they are true

Signposts

I slept through New Year's Eve, missed
the whole thing. No kiss, no ball-drop,
deep sleep near noisy Times Square.

Dream fragments went like this:
Familiar man emerges from shower mist.
Under a coarse thin beard, wrinkles show.

Floating over our bed, he sorts out playbills
from Shakespeare, Booth, Lincoln Theater.
We only remember details of a few plots.

Those plays are intense family dramas:
resentments, transformations, unexpected exits.
The pamphlets fall in stacks on fake rugs.

On top of each pile, I layer self-help books.
 "Be Gentle," "Practice Forgiveness," "Don't
Confuse a Long History with Everlasting Love."

Wake-up Call

Proud cocks crow in the Caribbean morn,
muezzins call flocks to worship,
lighthouse strobes flash danger.

We sleep with our backs turned,
knees drawn up like fetal snails.
I shut my eyes till the front door closes.

Discoveries bleed through dim-lit dawn:
questionable deals, memberships
cancelled, beneficiaries altered.

Back-and-forth retorts slice like rusty razor blades.
His clear blue eyes turn milky; my reflection
fades in a pock-marked mirror.

Sweet night connections end in crooked
sofa beds of separation. Cocks crow on;
the lark severs the throat of the nightingale.

Advent

I confide in the five I know I can tell;
their faces lose color, but not in surprise.
You are a survivor; we know you'll do well.

My sister, the constant, we sit by her fire,
describing strange dreams of the rupture to come.
Like others, she warns me, *Move slowly; it's dire.*

I've never known passion; I want to know now,
(too cautious, too careful, too thoughtful—I'm tired)
two years of weighing all options of *How?*

Dismayed that my mate is not more protective,
no questions, *How are you?* no offers to hold me,
the loss of an eye *seen from different perspectives.*

Sex fails—dilutes with the loss of mind-thrill,
too hard to mesh the urge and the dullness,
no carnal rise for a body stone-still.

Attempting to write a poem that's been written,
I hope to convince myself I can stay. But
my feet start to walk, they compose as I listen:

Say it in six words, a sestina.
Say it a lovesick way, a pantoum.
Say it in a sonnet, clever on line nine.
Or just say it—lob a free verse of chance.

I'm leaving.

2020 Upheaval

The mirror reflects my right eye, its falling lash;
my face appears old, but new, at every angle.
He removed my high school photo from its frame,
my sixteen-year-old skin so plump, no trace
of wrinkles, no signs of feeling downcast.
He placed this relic in a bag of mail, set it adrift.

A marriage, once vibrant, drifted.
One tries to recall joy and vow not to lash
out—only to practice kindness, not to forecast
disaster. One looks in vain for an angle
to find those evaporated feelings, just a trace
proving she once glowed in his silver frame.

I scan our pre-nup. It was a solid frame,
how sure we were we'd never drift
from life together. There wasn't any trace
of doubt. Until the gruesome accident ... I unlash
my fury at abandonment, my urge to strangle
his icy indifference, cold shock at being outcast.

Abruptly, life erupts. A novel virus recasts
health, families, the stock market into a strange frame.
Friends and enemies are forced to see conflicting angles,
problems impossible to solve must wait and drift.
Budgets, social life, school attendance are slashed,
invisible microbes shower us with little trace.

Desperately, we Clorox away unseen traces,
despair droplets in the Metro, slip on gloves to cast
away hidden germs, protect noses, mouths, eyelashes.
Learn to stay away, set our calendars to reframe
what seemed to be important meetings. Let drift
all dates. Forego commitments. Untangle.

The micro and the macro start to wrangle;
my personal struggle is a mere trace.
Terrified my strength to survive will drift,
I see the whole world may lose its casting.
I rail against a demagogue's outlandish frame;
only fools believe his "fake news" flashes.

Tracking time, we disentangle disrupted nests, reframe
our miniature traces in the whiplash of a world upturned,
broadcast bold dreams we hope won't drift away.

What to Expect at Congressional Cemetery

Not the graves that drew me there,
not the closed iron gates where I found an opening,
not the numbered maps leading to celebrity markers,

I turned to the un named, the no ones, the un knowns.

Confused by the totem poles along the brick walk,
distracted by the verse I was waiting for,
bewildered by grief and loss and heat,

I blinked through sweat, pulled my straw hat low.

Amused by the K-9 dog-walkers
who paid to be in the special society of cemetery donors,
we all were deciphering Washington DC anew.

Not the Cathedral School where my first husband taught,
not the Capitol Hill co-op where I lived for 14 years,
not the Annapolis flat I rented during separation,

I turned to hundreds of years of burying:

the 1892 epitaphs from husbands to wives,
tipped-back headstones of proud gay lovers,
locked vaults built by self-claimed venerables

made me flee back to the totems, the red carved cedars:

Female bear of liberty,
male eagle of war,
turtle in the middle of the crossbar.

I felt comfort from woodcarver, Jewel Praying Wolf James,
from Lummi Nation, a Washington far from Washington.
This is the verse I was waiting for, the distraction

I sought: all our arms linked underground
wrapped around one another, all our crooked
feet know pain and suffering.

Mother Earth holding us up,
Father Sun covering us down,
dogs and their owners keep walking.

A Wounded Pastoral

The truth is I yearn for a black tornado, something I can see
      spinning past the Monument,
        tearing up sod on the National Mall.

There *is* no sign of urban hubris, no suffocating traffic,
      only silent moms with mouth-scarves pushing prams,
        a few tourists walking six feet apart.

What was a two-mile expanse of mud patches and stubby grass
      trampled by families at Folk Life Festivals,
        scuffed up by sneakers of pick-up softball teams,

is the way-too-green lawn stretching all the way to the Capitol.
      I duck out of the Hay Adams for an hour in open air,
        walk by a Park Service mower lumbering past the Castle.

No one sits on benches except the homeless man with Tourette's
      shouting in spurts that Jesus will save,
        reaching into his battered grocery cart for a plastic bottle.

This has become the Not-So-National Mall for most are
      otherwise sequestered, sheltering in place;
        I clean my mask with sanitizer nightly.

No time for easy rest, my nightdreams vacant. I yearn for monsters
      I can see. No invisible germs. Avoiding folks is like heroin;
      it only works in the short term.

Running Refrains in Choleric Times

If I could buy insurance against death
then perhaps our social commitments could reappear:

>water cooler banter
>receptions for proud donors
>long-lost friends attending weddings
>soft Humboldt Fog cheese and Prosecco at poetry readings

If I could buy insurance
to abolish what were social virtues of the day:

>no one would work more office hours than their mates
>no one would strive to get more Facebook likes
>no one would count how many Plenary speeches she gave
>we would not care who visited the most exotic countries

Then, insurance against death might be affordable:

>take the coins off the eyes of travelers down the River Styx
>thrash away vultures circling our bodies
>extinguish touch deprivation from the universe
>grant everyone a smooth single malt

And the false decorum could end:

>we'd shake and hug with abandon
>wear loose velvet trousers and gold silky blousons
>lob outrageous compliments to strangers on the bus

Best of all, we could rejoice in
>being buried on our backs, headstones to the West
>feet pointing East
>we'd witness New Worlds Rising with the Sun
>no insurance needed

Digital Divorce

Zoom, a court of Hollywood Squares
Judge is *Host*
Participants in *Waiting Room*

Zoom, who will be there?
Admit   My Thumbnail appears
I've been muted

My lawyer and the clerk
row up along the top
Below   A Full-screen Judge

Pixelated all
wrangling *Audio* and *Video*
Up last   Opposing Attorney

Zoom, has 2020 come to this?
Solemn   Self-sequestered
Solo

Defendant   Not present
Invisible shadow of what went wrong
No parting words

Hands up for oath   Irreconcilable
Virus panic   Stock market free-fall
Vaccine questionable

Eleven minutes   Zoom for Decree
Zoom to mark QDRO Remote signatures
Twenty years   *Leave Meeting*

Essence of Blackbird

In the dreadful hour,
the Bird,
shiny black,
hovers.
Should I call
you Dark Omen,
who caws
damning messages?

Angel of sunrise
disguised,
you have come
to lift my heavy rings
and soothe my
sunken eye.
Why now, Old Bird?

Fluttering above my bed,
you brush my broken
wing, urge
me to hop.

You bring flocks
of calling birds,
who sing liquid
into my throat.
No longer restrained
by bedclothes,
I'm ushered by
feathers
to high roost.

From this perch
of silver air currents,
streams of white light
beckon radiant dawn,
shivering quills.

Strange Currency

If I could buy a sunset,
        I'd be rich in your scent—
a dusting of salt and black opium.

If I could purchase the memory,
        I'd wrap it in featherweight
lace to keep it almost intangible.

If I could retain the passion, I'd
        think of the moment I
blurted I love you and you responded.

Ever rich—I'd swim in the
        tenderness of amplified
feeling, up-breaths of excitement.

I'd replay the evening on the beach,
        your palms grazing my ribs,
smoothing down my hips.

For this, I'd pay a gazillion starfish
        and pocketsful of
doubloons that chime.

Castles in the Air

Make a blueprint of your dreams. Ready?

Sketch your palace on cream vellum paper, 100 lb. stock.
Give it the title *Newcastle* using your best handwriting.
Fold the page in thirds, shrink it to a miniature size
and seal it in a teeny mother-of-pearl box.
Wrap a 3-D printer in pink tissue tied with lavender ribbon.
Render that tiny too.

Cast a spell to lift you to the stars.

Wear a purple velvet jacket with side pockets.
Pack the miniature printer in the left one,
the mother-of-pearl box in the right. Strap a fanny pack
filled with dainty silver trophies around your tummy.
Rest horizontal on your pale aqua blanket
stuffed with soft cotton. Inhale. Exhale forever.

Whisper your mantra: Rise, rise, rise.

Float up through layers of stratosphere,
memorize names of colors as you drift by—
Hazelnut taupe, cabernet raisin, plum flan—
Choose *pêche-abricot* and slide in for a landing.
Plot on beaming up favorite friends and
invite them to Design Their Castle in the Sky.

They'll be wearing purple velvet jackets
carrying satchels of paint chips and mica.
Unpack your printer and diagram your doodles,
upload fanciful drawings into their minds.
Give gifts of amulets to spur magical ideas,
serve dulce de leche in mint-julep cups.

Introduce fantastic features—
Pietra dura walls of jewels,
beryl, garnet, peridot.
Balustrades of marbled mauve,
Windows, arched and tall, a drawbridge—
there are no rules of architecture for castles
in the air.

Leave your mark for hope and beauty.

Divorce Prayer: In Perpetuity Throughout the Universe

Compassion is the radicalism of our time.
The Dalai Lama

May joy be in this void
       without money, possessions, accolades.

May everyone have fulfillment—
       even you, even me.

Those who aren't skilled at happiness need it desperately.
       Don't diminish them, it takes nothing from you.

Greet your adversaries with prayers for peace.
       Then, chances for everyone's delight worldwide

are increased seven billion to one.
       Those are very good odds.

Thanks

I am grateful to the people who made this book possible:

my sister and first reader, novelist Betsy Woodman, my writing guru and co-conspirator since she was six and I was four

the magical visionaries at The Writer's Hotel and The New Guard Review: Founding Editor, Shanna McNair, and Consulting Editor, Scott Wolven

my mentors, critics and master poets: Grace Cavalieri, Chris Bursk, Sue Ellen Thompson, Alexandra Oliver, Sandra Beasley, Jane Rosenberg LaForge, Richard Harteis, and Leah Maines

my writer's group extraordinaire from whom I learn so much: Elizabeth Berg, Mary Mitchell, Donna Stein, Betsy Woodman

my steadfast supporters: Susan Clampitt, Jeremy Waletzky, Virginia Rice, Sarah Toth, Randy Wynn, Tanner Stening, Julie Jacobson, and Pete Chauvette

my generous instructors from The Writer's Center in Bethesda, Maryland: Judith Harris, Meg Eden, Nan Fry, Claudia Gary, Alexis Pope, and from Sun Magazine's conference, "Into the Fire": Sparrow, Sy Safransky

and to my publisher, Karen Kelsay, and the helpful staff at Kelsay Books

About the Author

Lee Woodman is the winner of the 2020 William Meredith Prize for Poetry. Her essays and poems have been published in *Tiferet Journal, Zócalo Public Square, Grey Sparrow Press, The Ekphrastic Review, vox poetica, The New Guard Review, The Concord Monitor, The Hill Rag, Naugatuck River Review,* and *Broadkill Review.* A Pushcart nominee, she received an Individual Poetry Fellowship from the DC Commission on the Arts and Humanities FY 2019 and FY 2020. Her poetry collection, *Mindscapes,* was published by Poets'Choice Publishing on January 9, 2020, and *Homescapes* was published by Finishing Line Press on May 22, 2020.

Woodman is a longtime artist and media producer, whose radio and film awards include five CINEs, two NY International Film Blue Ribbons, and three Gracies from American Women in Radio and Television. She worked for 20 years in leadership roles at the Smithsonian, was Vice-President of Media and Editorial at K12, Inc., and Executive Producer at Lee Woodman Media, Inc., with clients including The Library of Congress, The World Bank, Public Radio International, NPR, and the Fulbright Program.

An overseas childhood in France and India sparked Lee Woodman's love for language, art, theater, and dance.

www.poetleewoodman.com

Made in the USA
Las Vegas, NV
23 August 2021

28710620R00046